# A Practical Little Guide to Overseas Living

# A Practical Little Guide to Overseas Living

Joan B. Perkins

Copyright © 2017 by Joan B. Perkins
All rights reserved.
ISBN: 1542428750
ISBN-13: 978-1542428750

Cover photography by Joan B. Perkins

*For my partners in adventure:
Bill, Mark, Christy, Jessica,
Julie, Nathan, and Sam*

# Table of Contents

| | |
|---|---|
| Preface and Acknowledgments | 9 |
| Introduction | 11 |
| Chapter 1 – Preparing to Go | 13 |
| Chapter 2 – Getting on the Plane | 23 |
| Chapter 3 – Choosing Housing | 37 |
| Chapter 4 – Managing Food and Home | 45 |
| Chapter 5 – Handling Odds and Ends | 55 |
| Chapter 6 – Making the Adjustments | 61 |
| Chapter 7 – Studying History | 69 |
| Chapter 8 – Being a Learner | 73 |
| Chapter 9 – Showing Respect | 77 |
| Chapter 10 – Facing Social Issues | 81 |
| Chapter 11 – Returning to Home Base | 85 |
| Conclusion | 89 |
| About the Author | 91 |

# Preface

When one first makes a move overseas, there is a lot to figure out. It can be overwhelming and a little scary. I wrote this booklet as a simple and practical guide to ease the way for new travelers into the ex-pat world. Because I want this to be useful for those going to a variety of places, and because local circumstances can change rapidly, it is necessarily broad. It would be impossible for a booklet like this to be comprehensive. Therefore, this is more of a jumping-off point. Not every section applies to every place. Overall, I hope it helps your adjustments go as smoothly and painlessly as possible.

Joan B. Perkins
January 2017

# Acknowledgments

*A special thank you to Niloma Kolay French of* The Overseas Magazine *and Susan Lafferty for their suggestions and encouragement. Thank you, as well, to my fellow ex-pat sojourners, from whom I have learned immeasurably.*

## Introduction

Welcome to the ex-pat world! You will find that once you enter it, you become part of a community that includes military personnel, business people, missionaries, humanitarian workers, government workers, teachers, world travelers, and diplomats. Despite whatever causes us to choose the ex-pat lifestyle, there are commonalities we experience as we learn to traverse other parts of the planet than our own home base.

This little book gives ideas and suggestions for the adventure. Chapters 1-5 are longer and more technical in nature, with lots of lists and information. Chapters 6-11 cover broader topics, giving more general guidelines to think through or act upon.

While Chapter 1 deals with preparatory steps, some of these bleed over into Chapter 2, such as buying tickets and choosing luggage. You will also find a few prep steps scattered into the other technical sections, so please scan these parts of the book before you leave, just in case.

There are sections for notes after each chapter so that you can personalize it for your own circumstances. I hope you will mark it up and use it in the most beneficial way for *you*. Out of the more lengthy commentary, highlight the core information that applies to your situation. You might consider making a spreadsheet on your computer with the items that pertain to you, for easier recordkeeping.

As you head into this new lifestyle, I wish you safe travels!

# Chapter 1 – Preparing to Go

Before you get on the plane and begin your overseas venture, there are preparatory steps you *must* take, and then there are others you may choose to take to make your transition go more smoothly. Below are suggestions for getting ready, as well as some words of advice from what we have learned through our own and others' experiences.

## *Documents and Administrative Tasks*

If you are an American, peruse the U.S. Department of State websites in order to make sure your paperwork is in order, and note any warnings or other information about the country. Passports and visas can take time to obtain, so make sure you are aware of the schedule. If this is your first time to apply for a passport, on the application where it asks when and where you will be traveling, if you do not know the answer to that question, that is okay—you can still apply. Keep in mind that many countries will not allow people to travel in with less than six months left on a passport, so for all practical purposes, consider the expiration date as six months before the date in your passport.

Research visa information about the country as to what type of visa you need, for how long, and the steps needed to apply for it. Most companies and organizations with overseas workers help considerably with this. They should also help by advising you if there are other documents that must be acquired both before and after entrance into the country, in order to attain correct legal status.

Once you have your passports and visas, record expiration dates of both the passports and the visas in a place where you will be reminded to renew with time to spare. Staying on top of this can prevent some stressful and potentially expensive predicaments. Make photocopies of your passport and the appropriate visa pages to carry with you when you are traveling, in case of loss or theft.

Official birth certificates for each member of your family, as well as an official marriage certificate (if applicable), may be needed sporadically for various legal documents. Birth certificates will be needed upon renewing passports. These can be ordered from the state of birth and the state where your marriage took place. If you cannot find out ahead of time how many might be needed for any legal documentation requirements, take two to three copies per person, per document.

If you plan to drive while overseas, get an international driver's license to tide you over until you can get a local license. These can be ordered online. Basically, an international driver's license is a document verifying that your regular license is legitimate. It does not replace your license, but is a companion document to be kept with it. Read anything you can find about the traffic laws and practices in order to prepare yourself. Later, experience and observation will teach you much about the unwritten road rules of your new home. And the unwritten rules are extremely important!

Notify your bank that you will be moving overseas and need that noted on your account. They will be less likely to block your debit or credit cards for possible fraud, if your new location is in their records. Ask about international charges for the use of your debit and credit cards.

Pay off debts. Make a will. Name a guardian of your children in case of your death. Don't leave the legal matters for someone else to have to figure out without knowing your wishes. Legally name someone you trust as power of attorney to help out with any document signings needed while you are gone. Designate someone in your home country to handle paperwork and mail.

### *Medical and Insurance Preparation*
Check on immunizations recommended for the region where you will be going. Public health centers with travel clinics will have updated recommendations from the U.S. Centers for Disease Control and Prevention (CDC). Contact the nearest one well ahead of time to allow for proper spacing of vaccines. Some vaccine series can take

up to six months to complete the full series of injections required for immunity. You may need some series that are not common at home, such as rabies or Japanese encephalitis.

Take copies of your shot records overseas with you, but also leave copies in a safe place at home or online. In many locations, you will be in charge of your medical records, so you will need to keep a file of papers, lab results, x-rays, etc., in your home for future reference.

How will your health insurance work overseas? If it is provided by your company, will you pay and then be reimbursed? If you purchase insurance on your own, will the insurance company cover you internationally? If you are from a country with government health care, how do you process claims? Unless you are living where there is excellent medical care, you will want to check into insurance for medical evacuations. Will you need any local insurance, in addition?

Will there be any problems with your life insurance covering you in an overseas setting? Review your policy to make sure there are no restrictions on your location.

## *Personal Preparation*

Read up on the history and current events of your future home, in order to better understand the culture and the people. This may also help you avoid dangerous situations or assumptions. Read about the politics and religious tensions. If the country is English-speaking or you speak the language, read some of the popular writers of the country.

If there are local people from that country, befriend them and talk to them about their home. Ask *them* for book recommendations. Ask them if there are any authentic restaurants in your area so you can experiment with new cuisine.

Some people advise starting language study before you go. If your supervisor is suggesting it or you are very eager to start, of course you should do it. If you already have a good start on the language, expand on that. Otherwise, don't worry about it too much.

My personal opinion is that unless you have a great opportunity to do so, your time will be spent more efficiently in other types of preparation on the home front, and in language learning when immersed in the new culture. When you are actually in the culture, your need for language will be obvious. You will be hearing it and learning it with the local accents, dialects, and contexts. Living it will expedite your learning.

If you do not already know how to do so, learn how to cook simple dishes from scratch. Knowing the basics will relieve stress later. Many places do not have ovens, so learning how to cook on a stovetop with basic ingredients is beneficial. Few countries use the amount of packaged and prepared foods that the U.S. does. Practice buying fresh produce and meats, dried beans and rice, and making dishes that require no packaged products. If you have favorite spices that you are afraid won't be available, they are easy enough to pack in the corners of your suitcases. Make copies of your favorite recipes that do not require a lot of prepared ingredients. Some cookbooks are recommended in Chapter 4.

### *Material Goods*
Either through people with your organization, or through online groups, find out what is available and unavailable in your future home. Ask for suggestions of what you should and should not bring. Read the suggestions, but note that people's opinions vary greatly in what they feel is needed. Before you go out and buy all the suggestions you think you will want, be realistic about how much you may actually have room for in your luggage. You won't get this entirely right the first time you go, so try not to stress too much about it. You will take some things and wonder why you did, and wish you had brought other things. Perhaps later you can have someone send or bring in the items you wish you had brought.

Find out about clothes and shoes—are they available in your sizes? Particularly make sure any needed prescription medicines are available, though they may have a different brand name. Are there any items we take for granted, like antiperspirants, fitted sheets, or other commonly used products, that are not available, and that you would want to take with you?

Technology has made the areas of music and books much easier for the ex-pat. Now you don't have to take all the CDs and books that you think you will want for the next few years. An e-reader is helpful so that you have access to a more extensive library. Take digital photos of people and places special to you, so that you can reference them when you desire.

A laptop computer or a tablet is a necessity for most people, so ask if there is a service center for your favorite brand. In considering electrical appliances you might take with you, be sure to check on differing voltages and currents. Laptop computers and phones are generally made to work with both 110 and 220 voltages. (Get your phone unlocked before you leave, so that you can use your old phone with a new SIM card.) Some small appliances (e.g., hair dryers, razors) have models specifically made for dual voltage, but do not always work as well. A supposedly dual voltage curling iron with a little too much power can burn your hair right off, as I found out personally!

It is usually better to wait to buy large appliances in your new place. Then, you will know exactly how much space you have for the appliance, and you can find out which brands have local service centers.

If you are thinking about taking a family pet, research the laws concerning quarantine, vaccine certifications, and so on, for the country where you are going. Check into individual airline policies about transporting pets as well. It may not be wise or feasible, and the long flights may stress a pet considerably.

Most overseas moves involve tackling the material possessions one has accumulated over the years. It takes a lot of emotional energy to handle the sorting, selling, and storing of belongings. Do not be surprised if you find yourself grieving the things you realize are impractical to take or keep. You know they are just things, and perhaps not very important in the whole scheme of life. But they are *your* things, and may represent either your personality or important memories. The impact of getting rid of special possessions affected me more than I expected. More than once, I have been in tears through this part of the process. So if you struggle with this, you are not alone. Recognize the grief, take photos of items if you desire, and forge ahead.

At the same time, you can experience a real sense of freedom as you let go of material goods. Often, both extremes of feelings are mixed together, thus provoking the emotional and physical exhaustion of this aspect of moving overseas. An advantage to the periodic moves is that I have learned to fight my genetic hoarding inclinations, because the purging and packing is so painful and time-consuming. I never would have expected it earlier in my life, but I now feel joy in responding to the offer of something I don't really need with a simple "no, thank you."

## *Crating and Shipping*

Whether you crate and ship household goods overseas, or just take luggage and re-outfit once you are there, depends on many factors. Points to be considered:

- Cost of shipping

- Availability of needed goods in the new country

- Prices of goods in both the exporting and importing country. Is it cost effective to bring in, or is the item much cheaper in the new country?

- Quality of goods in both countries

- Whether your organization or company provides this service

- Ease or difficulty of importing goods

- Customs costs

- Emotional benefits of having your own things from your own country

- Emotional toll if those things are lost or damaged during shipment, or lost through an evacuation

- Stress of the packing, crating, and bureaucracy in getting the crate in.

We have done both, and find that initially we prefer to pay for extra luggage in order to have room for more items that make our life a little easier. Then we can outfit furniture and appliances once we get there. However, when we later moved between countries again, we preferred to ship our belongings (with the exception of appliances) due to difficulty in replacing our library and some furniture pieces. Obviously, there are pros and cons with either choice.

## *Details and Leave-taking*
Get the address and phone number (if possible) of where you will be staying upon arrival in your new country. You will need this information for immigration forms, as well as your U.S. address.

If possible, find out the generally accepted rate of airport tipping for your destination airport before you leave. When we landed in Bangladesh with *lots* of luggage (we had paid for extra), Bill wasn't thinking, and paid the typical American tip. We were rushed right through customs, taken to an air-conditioned office to wait for our ride, and offered sandwiches and cold sodas. We were instant VIPs! Since it was a strike day, we had been forewarned we would have to wait until after six o'clock for our ride. We were a little uncomfortable that we had overpaid so much and made ourselves even more conspicuous than we already were. However, that special treatment protected us a bit from the crowds and heat, and I was very grateful for that aspect of it. Most of the time, though, you don't want to make a spectacle of yourself like that!

Leave things in order—in relationships as well as the above-mentioned financial, legal, and material issues. As much as is up to you, don't leave with unresolved conflict or unexpressed gratitude.

When we had four children ages seven and younger, two of whom were baby twins, we had to move out of our apartment and put everything in storage before leaving Argentina for several months in the U.S. In the upheaval and stress of trying to get it all done and get ready to leave, we received some wonderful advice from a couple who had lived overseas for years. They told us that there is always more to do, there are more goodbyes to say, more last minute chores to handle, and you do what you can. But there comes a point where you just get on the plane. So "just get on the plane" became a slogan of ours when we became overly anxious about all there was to do, and the difficult goodbyes seemed endless. Just get on the plane! (The next chapter will tell you how to get ready for that.)

**NOTES:**

**NOTES:**

# Chapter 2 – Getting on the Plane

The move is going to happen, and concrete plans need to be made. From buying tickets, to landing in your next country of abode, it is time to get started.

## *Booking and Baggage*

When you have your passport in hand, with appropriate visas inside, it is time to book your tickets. Sometimes we have used a travel agent, and sometimes we have bought tickets online through a discount site. The advantage to using an agent is that they may have information you will not usually get online, such as which airlines provide complimentary hotel rooms for long layovers between flights.

Using either option, check the schedules carefully. It takes time to change planes, and if they are with different airlines, it may take a little longer. If the flight that you fly on into your final destination country is not your last flight of the trip, make sure you allow enough time to go through immigration and customs, and to transfer to the domestic terminal. Three hours is usually sufficient, giving you a little time to grab something to eat and freshen up if you want. "Usually" is a key word in that last sentence; when you are traveling, *anything* can happen, and it is impossible to foresee every eventuality. Do the best you can, and go with the flow on the rest of it.

At the time of booking, you should let airline personnel know of any special needs or meals. If you know ahead of time that a wheelchair will be needed, tell them. Meal requests for a child's meal, a vegetarian meal, or to accommodate food allergies can be made. Buying travel insurance is also done at booking. We didn't buy travel insurance for years, but at some point began to buy it. It does not cost much, but can save a lot of money if you have changes in travel plans or if other issues arise. If seat assignments can be requested at this time, go ahead and do that.

If you have metal plates, screws, or something similar in your body, get a doctor's letter explaining the situation, and make copies of the letter. Keep it with your passport, and notify security personnel before you pass through each metal detector.

If you are pregnant, most airlines have a point in the pregnancy after which they will not allow you to travel on their flights. This is usually somewhere around seven to eight months.

Look up the weight and size regulations for baggage, as well as number of allowed pieces, on all airlines you will be using during the trip. This includes checked and carry-on pieces. Note whether the number is referring to pounds or kilograms. Domestic flights usually allow for less than international flights, but if you are on either the same airline or a sister one, the airline sometimes allows the international baggage allowance to continue on for the domestic legs without additional fees. Be prepared to pay for fees if required.

Baggage allowances change often, so make sure you have updated information. Also check prices for extra bags, if they are allowed. If you will not be shipping a crate, an extra bag or two is really helpful!

Take changing time zones and dates into consideration. We forgot to look at that carefully one time; we wondered why the personnel at the layover hotel we had booked gave us such funny looks when we asked why the shuttle hadn't been there to pick us up. They didn't say anything though, and checked us into a room. We slept and went back to the airport for our flight the next morning. Bill even argued a little with the airline personnel when they said we were scheduled for a flight the *next* day. Then we found out the actual date. (We might have argued a little about that, too!) Thankfully, we were able to find a flight, and didn't have to wait another day, but it was a little embarrassing.

With changing baggage allowances for domestic travel, in the last few years we have found the 26" height size for suitcases to be preferable to the larger sizes. The smaller size is easier to pack without going over weight limits, the bags are easier to manage, and they usually fit domestic flight limitations as well as international ones. For awkwardly shaped objects, a trunk or plastic storage container works well, but the total dimensions should still be within the airline's designated allowance (you add height + length + depth to find your total inches).

Lightweight carry-on bags with wheels are helpful. You don't want to have to carry anything through multiple airports if you can pull it instead. And you don't want the bag to take up so much of the weight allowance that you don't have enough left for the contents.

We have often taken violins and guitars with us, and the airline usually allowed us to take them on board in addition to our allowed carry-on pieces. We have had to check a guitar at the gate, however, and it was damaged due to being in a soft case rather than a hard one. (If the airline personnel insist upon taking your instrument, assuring you that it will be fine, you do not have to believe them. You might not be able to do anything about it though.) Check with the airlines to see what their policies are for instruments.

### *Packing the Suitcases*

Once it is time to commence the actual packing, it is extremely helpful to keep a list of what is packed in each suitcase as it is being packed. I buy a small notebook specifically for this purpose. The larger your family, the more important this step is. (I do not do this for short or one-suitcase trips, but I *always* do it for the big moving trips.) Note the brand of luggage and its color at the top of that bag's page, because if your luggage is lost, the airline will ask for that information on the claim sheet.

With the list, if I needed something at the last minute that I had already packed, it was much easier to locate. Going through customs, with my list handy, I could answer any questions about what a particular bag contained. When we arrived at our destination, especially if it was a temporary stay and we did not want to unpack everything, I could locate any needed item without difficulty. A list could also help with any lost luggage or insurance claims.

It takes time to make the list, at a time when you may be stressed and rushed. However, having that little notebook has saved us a lot of frustration when trying to find specific things either before or after the trip, and has helped move us through customs easily. Even if you think you will remember where something is, by the time you go through all the packing and other preparations, it is often forgotten.

If you are traveling with another family member or members, spread some items belonging to each person among the suitcases so that if a bag is lost or delayed, each person still has some clothes and personal items available. If you will be staying a few days in a temporary place before traveling to your home, try to pack everything you will need for those days in one or two bags, so that you do not have to worry about lugging around and opening up all the bags just for those days.

Do not pack valuables in your checked luggage. This includes money, jewelry, cameras, computers, and other electronics, with the exception of something like a hair dryer. Do not pack official documents in checked baggage. It is too easy for your bag to be burglarized while it is going through the numerous bag checks, for it to be worth the risk.

As you finish packing each suitcase, weigh it and write that weight on your list for that bag. Try to get each weight close to the target weight until you are sure the weight on the last bags will not be a problem. It helps avoid extra repacking. Weighing the bags, and keeping the weight a pound or two below the limit, can save you the awkwardness and frustration of opening bags in the airport, and then trying to figure out how to reconfigure or decide what you should leave behind. It can also save money from having to pay overweight bag fees.

Put a card with your name and contact information in each bag, and make sure each bag has a nametag securely attached. When you are ready to lock the bags, use zip ties. TSA locks are great for traveling in the U.S., but overseas agents do not usually have the keys.

We have had several bags permanently damaged when the behind-the-scenes security staff cut through the zippers to check suitcase contents. The agents usually have zip ties, however, which they replace on the bag.

## *Packing the Carry-On*
When it comes to carry-on weight and extra bags like a purse or a briefcase, airlines vary in how strict they are. Most of the time, we have not had our carry-ons weighed, but there have been a few times when we did, and were required to check one at a gate in the middle of a trip.

Sometimes the weight issue is a matter of redistribution, and can be solved by packing a smaller fabric bag inside the carry-on in case you need to remove items to carry separately. If you still have to check the carry-on, you will be glad to have the smaller bag with the items you specifically need on the flight. My bag is large enough for my laptop computer, if I need to put it in there to avoid it being checked with the carry-on.

If the carry-on is boarded with you, it is nice to have the smaller bag that you can slip out of the carry-on for the duration of the flight. It helps you avoid having to pull the carry-on in and out of the overhead bin so often. You can slip the small bag back into the carry-on after the flight, and before walking through the airport. I usually keep a book, notebook, pens, toothbrush and toothpaste, comb, lip balm, and mints in mine. Travel documents go in my purse, which I can fasten more securely.

When our children were small, in their carry-on bags I would put their toys, activities, and snacks into a smaller bag they could pull out to keep in the pouch in front of them during the flights. I overestimated the number of toys they would need almost every time.

What you personally prefer to pack in your carry-on varies according to need and how risk averse you are. Below are items we take, and I have added some that I have heard others mention that they like to keep on hand:

- Any prescription drugs you might need those first few days. Keep them in the original containers in case there are any questions when you go through customs. Include inhalers and epi-pens, of course, if used by any family members.

- Motion-sickness meds; the non-drowsy type if you are responsible for someone else. Acetaminophen or ibuprofen; headaches are common when flying, due to dehydration. Antacids, because of airport and airplane food. An antihistamine, just in case, if you are prone to allergies.

- In order to help prevent getting sick from other people on the flight, some people take an immune booster occasionally throughout the trip.

- Small bandages

- Deodorant, toothbrush and toothpaste, razor

- Small hand cream, lip balm (the dry cabin air)

- Small pack of wet wipes

- Extra zip ties, in case you need them for your checked bags after going through customs.

- A small lock for the carry-on, in case you have to check it. A zip tie is not convenient, because then you will need scissors to be able to open the bag.

- The suitcase list notebook

- The cloth bag (or a large plastic zip bag for the kids' items)

- Snacks. Airplane meals do not always hit at the right times, and there isn't always time to remedy that during the layovers. A few packaged snacks can help tide you over between times. Extra points for those with protein to help you last longer.

- Breath mints

- A pacifier for babies, and gum for older folks, for those times when the air pressure causes ears to hurt

- Small toys and activities for children, including the favorite sleep toy or blanket

- Reading material

- Plastic bags, for a variety of purposes

- Copies of passports and visas

- Any travel or official documents (or these might be carried in a purse or briefcase)

- Compression socks

- A light jacket. You don't need anything that takes up much room, but airplanes often get cold once they get up in the air. Blankets are provided, but they do tend to be staticky.

- A full extra set of clothes. This takes up a lot of room, but accidents happen. The accidents aren't always yours, but can affect you and your clothes (thus, the plastic bag suggestion above). This can also come in handy if your luggage is late arriving.

For any children traveling with you, you might want to review their pockets and carry-ons before leaving for the airport. It is possible a favorite pocketknife that was a gift from a grandfather might make its way into the carry-on, and it might be removed by security personnel, which might cause some personal travel trauma. It is best to avoid this type of scenario.

After packing is complete, if someone on the other end of your travels will be picking you up, notify them of how many bags, including carry-ons and instruments, that you are bringing. That way they can make appropriate plans for transportation.

Tie a small brightly colored cloth, or place a strip of brightly colored duct tape on each bag to make it easier to distinguish your bags from other similar bags on baggage claim carousels. Always check the nametags before loading the bags up to take away, just to make sure they are yours.

## *General Hints and Information*

- If you can get boarding passes or seat assignments ahead of time, do so, especially if you are traveling with children. It can be taxing to be separated from a child who needs you—for you, the child, and the passengers sitting around the child.

- Store your passport and boarding passes carefully so that you do not lose them, and they do not get stolen. You will need to keep them close so that it will be easy to access them for any immigration forms you fill out while in flight; a pen will also be needed. Keep the photocopies of your passport and visa in a different location.

- Wear comfortable walking shoes. Airports can be large, and traversing them can involve long walks. These walks occasionally have to be fast.

- Wear comfortable clothes. You will be in them for a long time, and will want to rest the best you can on the long flights.

- Use layovers as an opportunity to get a little exercise between flights, if you have time.

- Stretch your legs, rotate your ankles, and generally move your feet around as much as is feasible. Get up occasionally and walk around. Some people like to wear compression socks on long flights as well. All these things help prevent blood clots caused by immobility.

- If your flight has individual TV screens, yours might not always work, so have some backup activities on hand. Our kids have had that occasional disappointment.

- Dehydration is common when flying. The air is dry, and trying to avoid having to go to the bathroom can cause you to not drink as much as you need. Drink water when you can. Try to balance out the soft drinks and juices on the flight with water, in order to avoid the extra sugar, which can make you feel sluggish. And you will probably feel sluggish enough without it. Layovers are a great time to try to get caught up on hydration if you are having trouble maintaining it on the flights.

- Be aware of your own body odors. When I asked some of my children what I should tell you in this section, they said that your feet can get really stinky. So be careful about taking off your shoes or socks without some pre-planning to keep the odor down. Your fellow passengers will be grateful.

- If you need money in one of the airports along the way for snacks or meals, you can either use your debit/credit card, or withdraw some local money from an ATM. There is not usually a need to carry much cash with you, unless you have been instructed to do so for items such as visa-on-arrival fees. If you are bringing in cash, find out beforehand how much is allowed.

- Long international flights usually have snacks of fruit, cookies, crackers, nuts, and candy, as well as water, coffee, and tea, available at the back of the cabin. If you get hungry or thirsty at a time when the cabin is dark and there is no food service, you can get up and help yourself.

- International airline food is often tastier than American airline food.

- You will be happier if you learn to be flexible when things do not go as planned. Flights get delayed or canceled, boarding passes fall through escalator steps, babies mess up all their clothes, and so on. Try to breathe deeply and take it as it comes, and one day it may make a great story.

- At some point in the trip, you may have some serious "Toto, we're not in Kansas anymore" moments. You get on a new flight, and the other passengers have changed from looking and speaking like those of your home country to those of other regions of the world.

- Make sure you check carefully for any belongings in and around your seats before leaving the airplane. This includes under the seats and the pouches in front of them.

- A note on traveling with children: Children who grow up traveling usually love it. Once our then two-year-old cried when we finished the fifth leg of our two-day trip because we were not going to get on another airplane. We had finally reached the end of a grueling trip. Airports feel like a mixture of home and adventure to them.

### *Security Checks and Immigration*

Make sure you make it to the first airport in plenty of time to go through the security checks. Three hours ahead of your flight is typically the recommended amount of time advised for international flights.

You may have to go through a security check or two for each flight on your trip. When planning airport meals or other activities, make sure you allow time for going through security and getting to the gate. Sometimes the gate is farther away than you anticipate. Remember that liquids don't get to go through security, so if you need water, either drink the whole bottle beforehand, or wait to buy it until after you have passed through.

When landing in a country you are passing through, you don't normally have to go through immigration unless you leave the airport. If you are going to a hotel off the airport campus for a few hours of sleep, or planning on participating in a city tour, be sure to allow time for going through immigration each way. In a layover country, unless you are planning to stay for a few days and have arranged to get your luggage, your bags are checked on through, and you do not have to pick them up or deal with them until you enter your destination country.

Immigration lines are often long, but they usually move quickly. If you are in a slow one and in danger of missing your next flight, tell someone who can move you up and rush you through.

Upon arriving at your destination, check your bags and musical instruments for damage before leaving the baggage claim area. Once you leave the airport, you may not be able to file a claim for damages. Normal wear and tear on bags is to be expected.

Going through immigration is usually done at the first airport where you land in your country of destination, even if it is not your final destination airport. After going through the lines and getting your passport stamped, you will normally need to get your luggage to take it through customs, even if you have checked it to your final destination. After customs, you check it back in for the last flight(s).

In some countries, the customs step is deferred until after the final flight. Do not assume it is one way or another, because then, you may either wait at the baggage carousel for luggage that never appears, or your luggage gets caught in no-man's land. They may not send it on unless you fly back and take it through customs, or until you fill out special government forms to get it. Ask ahead of time in that country. Airport personnel in your home country may not know how it is done there.

Oftentimes, airports have an indoor taxi stand where you get a taxi ticket before heading outside. This helps control the taxi traffic and keeps things more orderly. Taxis may cost more for fares to and from the airport.

## *Recovering from Jetlag*

Some people are not very affected by jetlag, but for some of us, it hits hard! From a west-to-east trip (U.S. to Thailand or India), it takes me a full week to recover completely. There is plenty of advice out there, such as taking melatonin, trying to stay up until bedtime, no naps, etc., that may work for you. I know they do help many people. For me, those things tend to only make me more miserable.

If possible, I prefer arriving around bedtime in the destination time zone, at the place where I can actually lie down and sleep, but most of the time it doesn't work out that way. In trying to recover a decent daily schedule, I try to sleep whenever I can and my body allows it, manage as many daytime activities as I can before crashing, and just wait out the week. I get rather disoriented by exhaustion, and can't sleep much on flights. If at all possible, I must sleep for a few hours when we first arrive, no matter what time of day or night it is.

It is very common for people to be doing well, and then all of a sudden they hit a wall and have to get some rest. You can actually see this happen when friends and family come to visit. Their eyes glaze over and you know they are gone. You can also feel it happening with yourself. You will be doing fine, then all of a sudden you cannot function and you feel your eyes rolling back in your head. Within a few days, your body has adjusted and you can manage life more normally.

Well, you are finally here. Welcome to your new home!

**NOTES:**

# Chapter 3 – Choosing Housing

When you arrive overseas, looking for housing is one of the first big challenges you may face. Questions you have never needed to consider in your home country can be very important. Sometimes, you are fortunate enough (or not, in some cases) to have housing already chosen for you. But when you have to find it on your own, here are some questions to guide you, keeping in mind that they will need to be tweaked according to the country, your job and purpose for being there, and your personality and needs. Find out what is standard practice in rental agreements and housing before you actually start looking for a home.

Some preferences will probably have to be compromised in order to satisfy issues you consider a higher priority. You may not be able to do anything about certain problems endemic to a country or area, but being aware of them ahead of time can help you be proactive, and thus minimize their impact. The answers to quite a few of these questions might be negative, but you will have thought through them and won't be walking into a situation unprepared. These are written from the perspective and experiences I had as an American living in South America, South Asia, and Southeast Asia.

While these questions may seem a bit overwhelming, especially if you have never had to think about these things, you will eventually take them in stride as simply part of learning to look at your new culture practically. This is a starting place, and maybe it will stimulate your thinking for the questions you need to ask in your particular area of the world.

### *Outside Considerations*
- Security if the house is a single-family dwelling and for some flats:
  1. Will you need to have a guard? (Do they usually live on the premises?)
  2. Is your entry/doorway easily accessible to the street, so that beggars, salesmen, potential thieves, etc., can ring your doorbell or case out the situation?
  3. Can people easily see when you are gone or when you are home?
  4. Can people reach in through your windows/window bars?
  5. Can a maid pass things from your home to an outside person through the windows when you are not looking?
  6. Can clothes or furniture be taken off your racks or through the bars from a roof or porch?

- What is the pollution level in the neighborhood (air and noise)? Is construction going on nearby? How will that affect the noise, dust and ability to get around?

- Is public transportation readily available (i.e., how far are you willing to walk in pouring rain or intense heat, or holding a sleeping baby)? If you have a car, your spouse may need it some days, or it may be in the shop, so these things should still be considered.

- How far is work from your home? What are the traffic patterns like?

- If you have children, is there a place for them to play?
  1. Are nearby parks relatively clean, and is playground equipment safe and in good condition?
  2. Are the park and playground free of stray animals?
  3. Is the play area in a place where your foreign presence would draw a crowd? (While in Bangladesh and India, our presence *always* drew attention.)
  4. Is there a club with facilities for children, if there are no playgrounds or play areas nearby?

- If a dog as a family pet is important to you, is there a place to take it for exercise and daily needs?

- Is the neighborhood a political hotspot where demonstrations are often carried out, or where riots take place during times of political unrest or on strike days? It may be fine to live in this area, but you need to know beforehand whether you should plan to work/play indoors during these times.

- Where are the nearest grocery shops and vegetable markets? (Preferably within short walking distance.) Do they have available most of the staples you need daily? Do they deliver?

- Is flooding often a problem during rainy season?

- Is this an area of frequent load shedding (electricity cuts) or water shortages?

- Talk to people in the neighborhood other than the landlord or real estate agent, if possible. It is good to go to the neighborhood without the agent, in order to walk around and get a feel for it. Then you can also see exactly where things are located in relation to the rental property. Visit the neighborhood at different times of the day.

## *Inside Considerations*
### *Security and Safety*
- Will you need railings for balconies (for either safety or security concerns)?
- Will you need a gate for the door(s)?
- What kinds of locks are on the outside door(s)?
- Are there bars for the windows (if needed)?
- Is there sufficient outside lighting?
- Is the electricity typically grounded in this area? (In Argentina, we had to make sure the refrigerator and microwave were grounded. A 220 electrical shock can be very dangerous.)
- If not, what do you need to do to ground it?

*Amenities, Comfort, and Possible Changes or Additions*
- Where does the sun hit in the a.m., p.m.?
- Are there sufficient plugs?
- If not, can you put in more?
- Are hot water heaters provided?
- Will you need to build kitchen cabinets? Will the landlord permit it?
- Is there a generator?
- How is the water system set up? (Are there outside lines or storage tanks?)
- If filtered or bottled water must be used, where can it be purchased?
- If cooking or heating gas is used, is it a built-in system, or gas cylinders?
- If cylinders are used for gas, are they in the landlord's name?
- If not, how long does it take to get an account and get it delivered?
- Are closets built in, or will you need wardrobes?
- Is the electrical system sufficient to consistently run the appliances you plan to use?
- Are light fixtures provided or will you need to install them? How much natural light is there?
- Are there good cross breezes?
- Are ceiling fans provided?
- Are there air-conditioners? Can they be installed? (You might prefer heaters where you live.)
- Is there a place for a washing machine (a plug and drainage)?
- Is there a place for a clothes dryer, if you desire and they are available (a plug and exhaust area)? Sufficient electricity to run one? Will you need drying racks—and where will you put them?
- Are curtain rods provided or will you need to install them?
- Can you install a shower rod?
- Can you repaint in the colors you prefer? (Can a paint job make it lighter, more cheerful, etc.?)
- Is there room for a home office if you need one?

*Possible Issues*
- Are there any stains from leaks or other damage?
- Is there puckering paint hiding a problem?
- Do you smell any mold or see any signs of it?
- Is the atmosphere depressing, and if so, are there ways it can be improved?

*Landlord, Services, and Contracts*
- If in an apartment building or complex, check out the elevators. How large are they? Are there service elevators for moving in and out?
- Is there any part of the house or apartment that you will not have access to?
- How are the utilities set up? (Electricity, gas, internet, cable, water, etc.)
- Does the landlord have preferred maintenance providers?
- Is the landlord local? If not, who will handle repairs, problems, etc., when they occur?
- Which of the above-mentioned improvements is the landlord willing to provide?
- How much is the security deposit? (What is typical here?)
- How long will the contract cover?
- If you need to move before the contract is completed, how much notice must you give?

## Advantages of an Apartment Complex

This may not be for everyone, but our lives were made much less stressful when we moved from the second floor of a three-story house in an old established neighborhood, to a newer apartment complex. The setting for this move was a mega-city in South Asia. These benefits would not have applied to our homes in small-town Argentina and in a neighborhood in northern Thailand, where a stand-alone house was typical. However, in the city, these things made a big difference for us:

- The complex was a closed community, so it limited the number of unknown people coming up and ringing the doorbell. This cut down considerably on interruptions to work and study time, eliminated most of our safety concerns, and helped make our home a much-needed haven.

- There was a central green and park area where our children could play and meet other children. This was especially nice on strike days when it wasn't wise to get out.

- Many people walked for exercise on the outer road inside the complex, either in the early mornings or evenings. It made a safe place to exercise and to meet people.

- Apartment complex employees dealt with most maintenance problems, and we were not personally responsible for finding a reliable person to come in and deal with plumbing and electrical problems. Nor were we reliant on the landlord to get repairs made. We just called the maintenance office and they sent the appropriate person.

- There was a generator system that provided at least some lighting and some fans when the electricity was out.

- When we were traveling, we did not worry about our apartment being broken into. It could have happened, but would have been much more difficult for someone to do than if we had lived in a single-family dwelling.

- There were grocery shops and drugstores conveniently located nearby, as well as produce stands.

- The flat was light and cheerful.

- Street noise and dirt were much less. We previously lived on a bus route, and noise and soot from buses were considerable.

- There was more of a sense of community with the other complex dwellers than we had in our former neighborhood, and it was much easier to meet them.

- We actually had more privacy than we had before.

Once you move into your new home, do whatever you can to make it feel like home as quickly as possible. It may take much longer than it would in your home country—hanging pictures on sheetrock goes much faster than hanging them on cement. But it will make a difference in how much of a haven your home becomes. I failed to do this in our first home in India; I never hung a picture in that apartment. When we moved from there, I realized how depressing our home had been. There were changes I could have made to improve the atmosphere. Armed with that knowledge, I was able to create a more welcoming ambience in later apartments.

**NOTES:**

# Chapter 4 – Managing Food and Home

Managing food and the home overseas can be quite different, and requires learning some new skills or adjusting some old ones. One of the most challenging adjustments is in the kitchen. Foods can cause us to experience homesickness like nothing else, because they are closely related to feelings of comfort, home, and culture. Dealing with food issues can be especially frustrating if you have never spent much time in the kitchen. You may have to work harder than you did in your home country to make sure you are eating healthily and getting the vitamins and nutrients your body needs. It is easy to let good nutrition slide when you are adjusting to so many things, but you will feel better and be less susceptible to illness if you make it a priority. The following is written from the American standpoint, but if you are from another culture, some of the tips might still be helpful to you.

### *Natural Foods Cookbooks*
Get some whole foods cookbooks—your old cookbooks full of regional recipes calling for all kinds of prepared or packaged goods will probably not be very useful. Natural foods cookbooks often not only have recipes, but also tips that teach you more about nutrition and how to adapt the recipes for the situation where you live. They are less likely to call for packaged products that are unavailable, but use basic foods and spices. If you will be in a place with good internet connections, I'm sure there are good recipe sites for whole foods. But if you prefer a hard copy, or want a variety of straightforward recipes all in one place, three very good cookbooks I have found helpful are these:

- *Whole Foods for the Whole Family: La Leche League International Cookbook*, Roberta Bishop Johnson, Editor. I have worn out two of these. This is a very practical book with a kids' section, a "making your own" section, lots of basic hints and instructions, and many delicious recipes.

- *More-with-Less Cookbook: suggestions by Mennonites on how to eat better and consume less of the world's limited food resources* by Doris Janzen Longacre. There are recipes from all over the world, with information on how to make the most of the resources available. We like the homemade corn chip recipe! The book emphasizes being responsible with foods and resources.

- *Rodale's Basic Natural Foods Cookbook*, Charles Gerras, Editor. A large book, it isn't as practical for packing. However, this cookbook contains not only many recipes; it is also a treasure trove of information about nutrition, basic food preparation and selection, and healthy eating in general.

Disclaimer: My copies are old editions, and I have not tried updated ones.

**Measurement Equivalent Lists**
Having information like the following in your kitchen makes conversions between American and other systems easy.

*Measurements (some of these are approximate conversions, but work for most recipes)*

Liquids:
1 teaspoon (tsp.) = 5 milliliters
1 tablespoon (T) = 15 milliliters
1 cup (c.) = 240 milliliters
1 quart (qt.) = approx. 1 liter

Dry:
1 cup = 250 grams (gm)
½ cup = 125 grams (1 stick of butter is about 125 grams)
1 lb. (of pasta, for example) = approx. 500 grams
2 lbs. = approx. 1 kilogram

*Temperature*
180 C = 350 F [conversion formula: (C temp. x 1.8) + 32 = F temp.]

## *General Tips:*
- All ingredients are not created equally in different countries. For example, butter may seem greasier, salt may be saltier, baking powder may or may not need to be doubled, flours may be more absorbent. Some of these things must just be discovered through experimenting.

- In American recipes, 4 eggs should equal approximately 1 cup, so if the eggs are small where you are, this is a guideline to follow rather than the number of eggs.

- In following recipes from your host country, note that the terms may not mean the same as the terms in recipes from your home country. For example, a "cup" may mean an actual typically sized teacup rather than an American measurement of 240-250 grams.

- In many countries, baking soda (sodium bicarbonate) is bought in the drug store or chemist's shop, and is not available at the grocer's.

- To make sure eggs are good, cover them with water. If they float, throw them away.

## *Substitutions:*
- Fats—oil, shortening, and butter may be used interchangeably in baking, but which one you use will affect the texture of the product somewhat. Oil makes brownies chewier, butter makes them more cake-like. In cookies that call for shortening, when you use butter overseas instead, you may need to add ⅓ to ½ cup more flour to make them firmer and less runny.

- If whole-wheat flour is finely ground, it can be substituted equally for white flour, but you may need to add a little more water or milk to the recipe to keep it from being too dry. It will change the texture and taste some, so you have to learn which recipes you like with more or less whole wheat. If the flour is coarsely ground, you may need to use white flour for a portion of the recipe in order to provide a better consistency of dough or batter.

- If you use honey in place of sugar, you need approximately ⅓ less honey for the same sweetness as the sugar. Again, it will change the taste and texture of the food somewhat, so you have to experiment to see which way you prefer it.

- 1 cup self-rising flour = 1 cup regular flour plus 1 tsp. baking powder and ½ tsp. salt

- For "Pet" milk or evaporated milk in a recipe, use powdered milk, but double the amount of milk powder you would use for regular milk. In some recipes, such as icing, you can use regular milk in place of evaporated milk.

- 1 square chocolate (1 oz. or 30 gm.) = 3 T cocoa + 1 T butter

- 1 cup corn syrup = 1 cup sugar + ¼ cup liquid (water) For dark corn syrup or molasses, use brown sugar. With either, add more sugar after the water is added and the sugar dissolved in order to make it equal 1 cup again.

- 1 cup buttermilk or sour milk = 1 cup milk + 1 T lemon juice or vinegar

- 1 cup sour cream = 1 cup cream + 1 T lemon juice or vinegar (Some people substitute plain, unsweetened yogurt for sour cream. Depending on how the yogurt is made in your country, using cream may give a smoother, thicker consistency.)

- Pancake syrup: 2 cups sugar, 1 cup water; heat together until sugar is dissolved. Remove from heat and stir in ½ tsp. maple or other flavoring.

- Chop up about a 200 gm. chocolate bar for the 12-oz. bag of chocolate chips for cookies.

## *Food Safety*
Clean vegetables and fruit of bacteria and parasites by soaking them in a water solution with a few drops of bleach or a few crystals of potassium permanganate for 10-20 minutes. Rinse with purified water and dry before storing. Do not store unwashed produce with that already washed. Vegetables that you will cook do not have to be soaked first. Fruit that has a peeling does not have to be soaked. However, if there is fruit with a peeling you plan to cut through, such as a melon, it is good to soak it so that the knife does not carry bacteria from the outside into the flesh of the fruit.

Dishes do not have to be washed with hot water (you may not have it in the kitchen). Just use plenty of soap. Make sure dishes and glassware are dry before using, to avoid water-borne bacteria. Use bleach to clean surfaces and utensils touched by raw meat.

## *Simplify.*
At first, I tried to recreate many of our favorite recipes. Most of them succeeded, but required a lot more work to make, since I didn't have frozen or canned vegetables, or other prepared foods. I learned to save the complicated ones for special occasions, and make most of our daily meals simple, but nutritious.

## *Keep on-going lists.*
Keep a list in your planner or phone of spices and food items that you cannot find locally, so that when you have the opportunity, you will know immediately what you need. I found it much easier to learn how to make things like vegetable dip and taco seasoning by using spices rather than trying to keep mixes on hand; it's healthier too! (We still prefer cooking this way now that we are back in the States.) The cookbooks mentioned above are helpful with this.

Vegetable dip: Equal parts sour cream and mayonnaise, garlic salt to taste, and Italian seasoning (oregano and basil) to taste. See the substitution list for how to make sour cream.

Taco seasoning: Use cumin and marjoram to season your meat to taste, and add some tomatoes (or tomato paste or sauce, if available).

Another list I make is one of the groceries we use most often. You can do this on your phone, or put it on the computer to print out and post on the refrigerator. I prefer the paper one, because sometimes the phone list is not accessible in a dead signal spot in the store. As I notice we need something, I simply circle that item on the list. If it is not on there, I write it in. Then when I head to the store, I don't have to try to remember everything—just the list.

### *Experiment with local products.*
Trying local foods will supply you with new favorites that you will look back on with fondness in the future. It will also make living in your new home less complicated, providing you with more possibilities for meeting nutritional needs. Ask national friends how they prepare vegetables that are new to you.

Sometimes you can substitute items that may not be quite what you are wanting, but will be "good enough." For instance, in our part of India, I could not find cornmeal for making cornbread. But I could substitute *sooji* (a coarsely ground wheat product) in my recipe, and though it wasn't quite the same, it was still good. I made walnut pies at Thanksgiving instead of pecan pies, using the brown sugar corn syrup substitution above. I found a vegetable similar to a sweet potato but with a purple peeling and a white center. I could substitute it in a traditional Southern Thanksgiving casserole, but it was much sweeter than our sweet potatoes, so I didn't need sugar. It was also white, so required a little brain shift when one was expecting the typical orange color.

The more quickly you can adjust to locally available foods, the easier it will be. However, there will probably always be at least a few things that you will want to bring in when you can. Our motto about those special foods was: Enjoy them when we have them, make do when we don't.

## *Household Hints*

Baby wipes can be made from a roll of cotton and water. If you have plastic storage bags available and are traveling, tear off pieces of the cotton, dampen them, and place them in the bag for easy wipes. At home, just tear off pieces of the cotton, dampen and wring out, and use.

Furniture polish can be made by mixing 3 T olive oil, 2 T lemon juice, and water to make 32 oz. of polish. Shake well before each use.

Roach killer: 8 oz. powdered boric acid (can usually obtain from chemist's shop), ½ cup flour, ⅛ cup sugar, 1 small chopped onion, ¼ cup shortening or bacon drippings, water to form soft dough. Mix together into a dough-like ball. Pinch off pieces and place in areas where roaches come in. WARNING: Wash your hands immediately after touching. Do not place where pets or small children can reach, or where it might contaminate your food. We lost two guinea pigs due to this dough. We did, however, find it much better than using the pesticide company, who drenched the whole apartment with spray. And it was quite effective.

Homemade electrolyte drink #1: 4 cups water, ½ cup orange juice (or other fruit juice), ½ tsp. baking soda, ¼ tsp salt, 1 heaping T sugar.

Homemade electrolyte drink #2 (Bill likes this after his long runs.): 2 lemons, juiced (and/or orange if you have one), ⅓ cup honey, ¼ tsp. sea salt, water to make 1 quart.

Search online for "homemade (whatever it is you need)" and you might be surprised by the options, from toothpaste to insect repellant. Then depending on your local available ingredients, choose what you can make yourself to substitute for the things you cannot find on the shop shelves. If you do not have available internet, start a list of the household recipes you need. Then when you are traveling to an area where you have internet access, download the recipes for the household products you haven't been able to find so that they will be accessible when you get back home.

In tropical and subtropical areas, you will need to store some food items in the refrigerator or freezer that you might normally store in a pantry. This helps protect the products from insects and the effects of heat.

### *Household Help.*
In some countries, hiring household help is common. In fact, it may even be seen as selfish if you could provide a job for someone and you refuse to do so. For independent Americans, this can be a difficult adjustment. Most of us are not used to having household helpers, and are not comfortable with a service-oriented culture. Yet, because the cultural adjustments are so great, and life responsibilities take up so much more time, we find that we need someone to take tasks off our hands that we used to do for ourselves.

If you are interested in hiring household help, talk to national friends and neighbors to find out what is typical in the area and among your social level as far as salary, holidays, job responsibilities, and so on. For us, personally, we wanted to pay a good and just rate, but not a rate that would make us stand out as ridiculous or foolish. We wanted to treat them on the high side of fair, but still have someone who would do the work we needed to get done. We wanted to treat them with respect and kindness, but not to be so chummy they failed to respect us.

In many countries without a strong social service system, you, as the employer, might be expected to help with medical expenses or may be asked to help out with a loan in a time of crisis. It may go beyond the employee to their family members, as well. In India, it was interesting to see that many national employers might not pay as well as we felt we should, but would tend to be more generous in a time of crisis than we were naturally inclined to be. It is good to think through what you are willing and able to do in these areas ahead of time. It sometimes takes experimenting to find a balance that is healthy for both parties.

It may take you some time to learn how to function in this new environment. Don't be afraid to experiment in the kitchen—though you might want to do it before you try it on guests! You will have some failures, but before long, you will be much more comfortable, and it won't seem so overwhelming. You may make some mistakes with household help. But you will learn, and that, too, will become less burdensome.

**NOTES:**

# Chapter 5 – Handling Odds and Ends

There are a few odds and ends I want to mention before we move on to the more general chapters. These do not fit easily under the other topics, but might be helpful or necessary for you to consider.

## *Education for Children*
If you have children, you will need to have educational plans. Options vary considerably depending upon location, so ask lots of questions of anybody you can who knows about the particular schools you have in your area:

- International schools are often cost prohibitive unless your organization foots the bill. They can be great or not so great, both academically and socially. Find out what you can ahead of time if this is one of your options.

- Mission schools are also often international, but may be much less expensive. They also vary in quality. The one our older children graduated from was excellent, and did a great job preparing our children for college. These schools may have a mix of students from business, diplomatic, and missionary backgrounds, and from a variety of countries.

- Public national schools may be an option, depending on the local laws and school quality. Language may be an issue at first.

- Private national schools could also be explored. Our oldest child went to one of these for a while when he was quite young, and it was a good way to learn language and make friends.

- Online schools, at least for upper grades, are becoming more and more common. Some students work well using these, and others find they need more hands-on guidance and interaction.

- Homeschooling can be a good fit for many families, especially as you don't have to worry as much about conflicts of scheduling when you face required visa runs or conferences. It can provide some educational stability within a mobile lifestyle. In some countries, this may be illegal; in others, while not legal for citizens, it might be an option for foreign children. In the countries where we have lived, it was not a problem.

- Boarding schools, either in your own country or a neighboring one, have sometimes been a big help to families living overseas. Some students respond well to a boarding school environment, and some do not.

Which option is best may change as a child grows and develops. It can vary within a family, depending upon the individual child's needs and personality. It's okay to realize something is not working and needs to be changed.

When considering schooling and activities for children, it is sometimes difficult to determine what is best. You want your child to love the culture, have deep friendships, and learn the language well. Yet, it can also be very important for your child's identity to be able to move back into the passport country's culture with as much ease as possible, and to know the passport country's language well. There will be bumps in determining proper balance. We tried to keep in mind both these views: this is where they live now, and they need to be invested; that is where they will live later, and they need to be prepared for it.

If your child needs educational testing for learning disabilities, there may be a regional organization that does this for ex-pat families. Ask around and do some internet research to see what you can find out for your part of the world.

ACT and SAT exams are usually offered at the international schools. They may also be given at your embassy or consulate, or at an American center in your region.

Residency status in your home state may need to be maintained for the purpose of in-state college tuition. Research your own state's policies for this. Maintaining your U.S. driver's license, filing income tax in your state (even if you don't owe any), and maintaining a U.S. address if possible, can aid in this process.

## *Tax, Financial, Legal, and Contingency Plan Issues*

Research whether you will be required to file and pay income taxes in your home country, your adopted country, or both.

You may need to set up a bank account with a local bank to handle local transactions.

Find out how much money you can get out each day from an ATM. Many times, there are limits. So if you have a large cash expense coming up, you have to plan ahead so you will have sufficient cash on hand for the bill.

Stay up-to-date on the documents you need for being in the country legally.

It is often recommended for American ex-pats to keep a certain amount of U.S. dollars in cash in a home safe, in case of emergencies where evacuation may be required. Contingency plans may call for necessary and important documents (passports, birth certificates, etc.) to be kept in a place together where they can be gathered quickly, yet kept safe from theft or damage when not needed.

Naming a person in-country to have temporary guardianship of children in case of parental accident or death is wise.

If you plan to marry a person from your adopted country, consult immigration lawyers in both home countries to determine how immigration law will affect your marriage and your future children. Which country is best to actually be married in? How will where you are married affect future visa and residency issues? How long does it usually take to get the proper visas?

If a child is born to you while you are overseas, check with the U.S. Department of State site to determine what you need to do to register the birth as a U.S. citizen born abroad, and apply for the child's passport.

Soon after your arrival, register with your home country's nearest embassy or consulate so they know you are in the country, in case of emergencies and crises. A reminder note should be made for absentee voting through the embassy or consulate. Overseas voting must be done in advance, and the deadlines for registry come early.

### *Short Trips*
When you live overseas, there are often short trips you must take from time to time, such as for visa runs, vacations, or meetings. Some visas require that you stay in the country no longer than 90 or 180 consecutive days at a time, for example. For these shorter trips, I kept a folder on my computer with a packing list for each child and myself. For each trip, I would pull up the lists, adapt them for the upcoming trip, and print them out. Once a child could read, I would give them their own list, and they were responsible for packing and checking off the items on the list. We parents were responsible for all important documents, of course. This helped me a great deal, as well as taught them responsibility.

### *Journaling*
If you like to journal, your overseas experiences will provide great material. If you don't like to write, try your best to document your experiences in some way—photos, or perhaps word lists—something that will help you recall them. While you are sure you won't forget the interesting incidents that you face, many of them are pushed from memory by more pressing issues. Being able to go back, see, read, and remember details of events, brings back feelings and impressions that make them all real again. Even when you have been overseas for years, now and then stop and just *look around you*! Isn't it amazing that you are here, living this life?

**NOTES:**

# Chapter 6 – Making the Adjustments

Oh, the adjustments. Sometimes it's the little ones that just about drive you insane. How do you do it? What are the things you can do to ease them?

***Get out and explore.***
The more quickly I can manage getting around, the more quickly I feel comfortable in a new culture. I am an introvert, and when I am overwhelmed by all the changes, it is a challenge to make myself get out. However, knowing my area and orienting myself to where various places are located go a long way in helping me feel more at home in my new place.

When we moved to Thailand, I had one week with my husband there before he had to travel. We got groceries, driver's licenses, maps, and trash cans. And then he left. My older kids were old enough to leave in charge of the younger ones, and none of them were too keen on riding around while I continued with the numerous errands necessary to help us settle in well.

So I got in the car and got out in the town. And got lost. And got lost again. (I didn't have GPS back then, but I did have a good map.) However, when I got lost, I also figured out where I was and how to get back home. It was amazing how quickly I went from feeling overwhelmed to growing confidence each time I found myself heading back into familiar territory rather than into another province! You do want to find out quickly which areas to avoid, for safety and security reasons.

When we first moved to Kolkata, our family went out on field trips every Friday for about six months to explore the local tourist sites. Even many years later, we have fond memories of our experiences during that time. It helped us not only find which places were fun for us and for visitors, but it helped us learn something of the history of our city.

### *Meet your neighbors.*
This is not always possible, but when it is, it can help you feel more at home. Neighbors can advise you on the best places to shop and eat out, which brands to buy, and which doctors to see. It helps build relationships when they see you coming to them in humility rather than with sometimes-typical foreign arrogance.

Knowing your neighbors can help you feel safer, because you have someone to call on in an emergency, or someone to ask questions who knows your area. I know there are exceptions, but most people will want to help you if they realize that you are sincere in your efforts to get to know them. I am referring primarily to national neighbors; while ex-pat neighbors can be a big help, making friends of nationals will help you settle in more completely.

### *Find the perks.*
Look for the helps that might not be part of your life in your home country. Household help might be affordable—and needed due to homes getting dirtier faster, cooking and marketing taking much more time, and personal duties being more demanding.

Often, shops and grocery stores deliver to your door. So might the chemist (pharmacist). In some countries, little family-owned restaurants provide meals cheaper than you can cook them at home. The local ironing man picks up your clean clothes and returns them freshly ironed. Keep your eyes open to see what conveniences around you can make life easier to manage. Then take advantage of the ones that appeal to you.

### *Get involved.*
In order to get to know people and get out into the community, look for ways to get involved. Work may be so all-inclusive that it doesn't leave time or energy to add other activities, especially at first. However, keep your eyes open for possibilities. Join a civic club, a choir, an orchestra, a church, or a book club. Attend a cooking class or an exercise class. Often, even an introvert can find things to do that are not too demanding time-wise, yet provide venues for meeting people and helping you feel more connected socially.

## *Recognize culture shock.*
Culture shock is common, and there is no need to feel ashamed or be in denial when it hits you. There is also no need to feel proud if it doesn't. It is perfectly normal to have moments or days when you ask, "What in the world have I done?"

I asked that question on the way from the airport, when we landed in Dhaka, Bangladesh, for the first time. It was followed by the forlorn thought, "We had a nice life in Argentina." Exhausted and overwhelmed, I was looking out the van window as we drove down the streets, tears sneaking their way down my cheeks. I also asked that question when I lay in bed at night, feeling the tremors following an earthquake we experienced the first month we lived in Costa Rica.

Culture shock waxes and wanes, so don't be dismayed if it catches you by surprise some days. A couple of days later you may be doing great.

## *Know your limits.*
Learn when it is time to take a home day (or an office day) and stay in your comfort zone. Some days you need to *not* be challenged so that you can get some soul rest. A little can go a long way as you are restored by a good book or some time with a quiet hobby or cup of tea. Even taking care of paperwork in the office can be restorative.

With family or friends, watching a funny movie together or having a game night can help soothe stressed personalities. Laughter really is good medicine, so if you can facilitate that, it is healthy for everybody. Sometimes, amid the tensions, we forget to have fun.

You will have frustrations and will probably have "I hate (name of country)" days. Just try not to run out in the streets shouting that, okay? Be patient with yourself as well as with other family members. People adjust and adapt at different rates and in different ways. Playing the comparison game doesn't help. Sometimes the adjustments seem to be going well, and then culture shock and homesickness circle back around.

Overall, it takes time. The first time I moved to a vastly different area of the U.S., I cried on a visit to my mother, "Why can't I adjust?" I have learned since then that I usually adjust fairly quickly on the superficial level. Yet, it generally takes me about three years to adapt deeply. I have to accept that and be patient with myself, doing what I can to stay connected with people. (Have you noticed that frequently recurring "be patient" theme?) Even when you are well-adjusted and comfortable in your adopted land, there will be occasions when you get homesick, especially if you have loved ones back in your homeland. That's normal.

Flexibility is important. Balance is important. For example, social media and being able to stay in touch with family and friends through technology is so much easier these days than when it took weeks for mail to travel back and forth. But if you spend all your time online with people "back home," it will prevent you from being present where you are, and from learning to depend on the people where you now live. The new friendships need space to develop and grow.

Be generous in spirit toward other ex-pats. When someone else's coping tools vary from your own, it is easy to be critical and judgmental. Yet, they may be far ahead of you in another area. You do not know what challenges a person may be facing both here and back home. Show kindness, especially keeping in mind that you may need it shown to you before long.

When frustrated due to the lack of a hobby, instrument, or sport that you previously enjoyed but which is impossible to do in your new home, look at it as an opportunity to learn something new. I didn't have a piano, so I decided to learn how to play the violin. It satisfied that need to express myself musically, and I got a lot of joy out of it. Bill always missed watching football, basketball, and baseball during their respective seasons, though he managed to watch online college football very early some mornings. However, he also gained an appreciation for cricket and soccer.

Learning to deal with bureaucracy is a vital skill for the ex-pat, especially in developing countries. Make friends with filling out forms. The sooner you can learn to relax about it and realize bureaucracy is simply part of your new lifestyle, the better off you will be. Take a good book along to government offices. Related to this is the fact that in many countries, you will not be able to accomplish the same number of tasks in the same amount of time as you did in your home country. Unrealistic expectations about what can be accomplished in a day can cause you a lot of distress, so give yourself some grace when it comes to your checklist.

Living in a foreign culture can be stressful, and can cause issues to become very large, very fast. Pay attention to how you and your family members are handling the pressures. Sometimes we were trying so hard to make it, that we were not in tune with underlying struggles within our family—even our own struggles, as the parents. I can look back and say, "Oh, we should have done this, or that," but at the time it was hard to see, and I was overwhelmed.

Get help if it's needed—before things escalate too far. Prevention is easier than rescue. Our organization had counselors we could call or chat with online, and they were a lifesaver for me at various points along the way. In addition, I had some friends I could turn to (and cry with), and they could do the same with me. I know that isn't always possible in the flesh, but be proactive in seeking help through online options, if needed. In these days, you are not limited to only those people and helps within physical reach, so don't stop looking just because you cannot find local counselors available.

### *Holidays*
Holidays can be hard to face overseas. You may live in a country where the holidays that are most special to you are not celebrated at all—either because they are national holidays of your own country, or because they are religious or cultural holidays.

While a range of emotions would overcome me during special holidays—homesickness, sadness, loss, anticipation of how it would be that year—at the end of the day, most of the time we had found some way to make the holiday special or have new meaning.

When we first went overseas, I remember saying, "I know that Christmas is commercialized in the States. But I *miss* the commercialization!" Over time, I began to appreciate the simpler Christmas traditions our family developed. We were able to focus more on the true celebration than the cultural trappings of it. I enjoyed the more over-the-top celebrations when we were in the U.S., but would long for our pared-down overseas versions at the same time.

There are times when you will want to celebrate holidays with your ex-pat friends. Other occasions, you may want to introduce your national friends to your festivals. Either way, while you may not be able to fully recreate a holiday as it used to be for you, you are making memories and new traditions that will be special for you and your family.

**NOTES:**

**NOTES:**

# Chapter 7 – Studying History

I mentioned in Chapter 1 that you should study the history of the area that will be your new home. This is a good practice to continue once you are there. The more you learn about what has happened in the past in the country or region where you live, the more the present will make sense. Understanding the past will help you be more effective in your interactions with the people of your new place.

One day, I was making a few culturally insensitive remarks to an Argentine I met on the street. (I have no idea now why in the world we had this discussion in the first place!) "Why don't Argentines try to save their money? They wouldn't be in such financial difficulties if they would look ahead to the future."

The woman to whom I was speaking angrily gave me a full-on lesson in the importance of understanding history: "You didn't live here in the days of hyper-inflation! If people didn't go out and spend their full paycheck on the day it was received, they didn't have anything to show for it, because in a day or two, the value had dropped to almost nothing. If they saved, they lost everything! It's kind of hard to put that behind you." Well, that was humiliating, but was one of my first deep realizations of how history shapes who we are and how we act.

As you study, research the answers to questions such as these: Who were/are the oppressors, and who were/are the oppressed? What is the religious history and how do its tenets influence daily life? How has the country's economic development impacted the individual's choices?

Look at the tensions between groups and ask, "Where did these come from? What happened in the past between these groups and why?" Ask these questions of your own culture to help you understand yourself and why you look at life differently from those of your secondary culture. Take it even further: Go from the country's history, to the region's history, to the city's history, to the ethnic group's history, to the family's and individual's history.

While living in Kolkata, neat traffic lines were non-existent. You could rant and rave about the lack of orderliness, but it wouldn't do much good. Look at history—for example, the history of the taxi drivers: Many of the taxi drivers came from poorer states outside of West Bengal. They were from backgrounds where one had to fight tooth and nail to meet daily needs. If you didn't scramble and compete for everything you could, you were pushed aside and needs went unmet. So you learned to push and shove and grab out of self-protection. Put that on the road now. See how that affects traffic patterns?

The more you can learn of history and how it has played out in both your own and your adopted cultures, the more you will be able to develop a heart for what makes the people who they are, and the more you will appreciate how they handle life. You still may not like it, but you will at least be able to understand some of the whys.

Keeping up with history as it is occurring, through staying up-to-date on current events, is also important. It can keep you safer as well as give you a way of connecting with the people. The local newspaper can notify you of strike days, cultural events, sports events, and keep you informed of local politics. Especially if you live in a volatile area of the world, staying aware of any growing tensions and hotspots can be vital to your safety. Even if you do not live in that kind of area typically, it is wise to keep your finger on the pulse of what is going on around you.

**NOTES:**

# Chapter 8 – Being a Learner

Many times when a person heads to an overseas appointment of some kind, that person goes in order to offer something to the overseas culture. So there is often a sense of pride or even patriarchal benevolence toward the culture from the beginning. This can be a hindrance in building meaningful relationships, whether they are business, humanitarian, or personal relationships.

There truly may be something you can offer which your new home needs. Otherwise, you might have been better off staying home. So this is not denying that you can contribute. However, do not neglect to realize that your new home has things to offer you and teach you, as well. Be humble, and learn what you can!

I knew that my husband had earned respect from many in our home of Kolkata, India, because he was a learner of people and the culture. But on a train trip a couple of years ago, I saw firsthand one of the reasons why. We were traveling with a large group of people, so there was a lot of milling around and visiting among the group. One of the young men came and sat down with us for a time.

Bill, who was old enough to be his father, began to ply him with questions; not the type of questions meant to badger, manipulate, or force an agenda, but the type of questions that respected the knowledge and expertise this young man had of his own culture and people. We learned from his insight and the sharing of his knowledge and experiences with us. I was thankful to be married to a man who genuinely wanted to learn, and who was not hindered from doing that by focusing on bestowing his own knowledge.

Other ways that you can be a learner include learning the music, how to cook local foods (or at least enjoy them!), how to make local crafts, and how to use the language effectively. I feel a bit hypocritical emphasizing language, because I never became proficient in

Bangla, the language we studied for living in Kolkata. But even what I did know helped me understand the people better, and drew them to me because of my interest in their culture. I knew from learning Spanish that the language teaches you more than just the words people speak, but also their patterns of thinking. You will find yourself greatly enriched if you place yourself in the role of student of the culture.

Learn about the local festivals, both religious and national or regional. How did the festivals start? How are they celebrated? What significance do they have on the personal level?

A not-so-lovely part of being a learner involves learning to be streetwise for your particular new culture. Perhaps it was safe to leave items out on a porch or in a yard in your former home, but it tempts thieves in your new one. A bag slung over your chair in a restaurant might have been safely left alone before, but is in danger of being stolen in this culture.

You may need to learn how to carry yourself so that you do not look like an easy target. We taught our children to always be aware of the people around them, to walk confidently with an air that lets others know they know what is going on. For their protection, we learned to walk behind our daughters whenever we were in a public place. You must find out when and where it is safe/dangerous to be out in your new home.

Learning to read people and their cultural cues will be to your benefit, as well as learning whom you can trust and whom you should be slow to trust. The biblical mandate on being both wise as a serpent and gentle as a dove comes to mind.

**NOTES:**

# Chapter 9 – Showing Respect

When you move into another culture, there are things you will usually love about it, and things you will not so much love about it. It may take a little time for those to show up and define themselves, or it may not. Vital to making the most of living in another culture is treating that culture and its people with respect. Respect the laws. Respect their manner of dress as far as what is considered modest and decent. Respect the manner of "being" of the people (e.g., perhaps they are generally quiet when your tendency is to be loud and boisterous).

Treating a culture and its people respectfully doesn't mean that you cannot be clear in your mind about those things that are obviously wrong, such as sex trafficking or mistreatment of others. But culture-moving often brings stages where you just think these people are crazy or stupid, and you cannot see that those areas that annoy you the most may not cover moral issues, but cultural habits.

When we first moved to Argentina, I was a young housewife, and I was irritated at the way the women mopped their floors. It sounds silly now, but it seemed like a big deal back then. I said something to myself like, "I will never mop that way!" At some point, I saw that using a damp floor cloth flipped over a squeegee was a much quicker and more efficient way to clean than my American-style mop.

Also in Argentina, in January each year, I found that it was typical for the stores in our little town to run out of ketchup. You can see that I was concerned about the important things in life. It was so aggravating that the people in the factories took the very hot month of January and/or February off for vacations and such. Why would they do that? Didn't they understand how much profit they lost by not keeping ketchup on the shelves for people like me who hadn't known to plan ahead?

As the years passed, however, I saw how wonderful it was to be in a culture that valued time with family and friends above the almighty dollar. This also applied to time in the middle of the day for siestas, when children came home from school for lunch, and shops were closed in our town. I eventually saw that it was a better use of time to take a break during those hot months and times of the day anyway, as productivity was at its lowest then.

It is easy to see how cultural misunderstandings can take place. You might wrongly assume from the second example that the Argentines were lazy or had no business sense. Actually, they simply had their priorities in a different place. It is wise to hold back judgment in areas that do not involve moral affairs, and learn to respect that your new culture has its own reasons for doing things its way. You may even find yourself adopting some of those ways as your own.

In showing respect, be slow to openly criticize the country, its leaders, the culture, and so on. Be observant, of course, but your spoken criticisms may only harm, and not help improve anything. Nationals may agree with you, to a point, but may also be hurt or offended by your views or complaints. It's hard not to fall into complaining and criticizing when in the throes of culture shock—most of us ex-pats have failed in this way at some point. Remembering how it might make a national feel can help temper those responses.

Studying history, being a learner, and showing respect are all very closely tied together. If you want to be an agent of change, be very careful and respectful in how you go about it, making sure your motives and methods are above reproach.

**NOTES:**

# Chapter 10 – Facing Social Issues

Beggars are rampant in many countries. Gut-wrenching poverty is real. Balancing mercy and wisdom can be difficult and sometimes emotional. There is a wide range of how ex-pats come to peace with their responses to it. Some ideas:

- Carry food or snack bags in your car or backpack to give when approached. Some people will only want money, but others will be grateful for the food.

- Support those who are poor but working, by buying goods or services from them, even if you might not need the goods or services (e.g., children selling gum, the shoeshine man).

- In bargaining, make sure you are still being fair to the seller. A few cents' difference might mean a lot more to them than it does to you.

- Support in some way an individual who is unable to work, perhaps by providing an occasional meal or by giving coins periodically.

- Be okay with being taken advantage of sometimes—you won't always be able to discern between a true need and a very good actor.

- Trust your gut. Sometimes we went against our usual practices because we felt we should.

- Find local reputable benevolent organizations or individuals to support.

- When you have hired help of some kind, pay the upper end of what is normal locally.

- In doing any of the above, try to guard your attitude and not be patronizing. Those attitudes are easy to read, and yet, the person may have no choice but to accept what you give no matter what your attitude.

### *The Orphans*

When living in the cities of this world, we are faced with the question, "What about the orphans?" So many kids need to be cared for and loved. So many kids are ripe for being trafficked. Maybe they are not officially orphans, but emotional and/or physical ones.

Some Americans, first realizing the widespread needs, assume it's fairly simple to adopt a child, or take a child into their home, when they live overseas. Sadly, can be very complicated. Countries have their specific adoption laws that vary from those of other countries. Some countries do not allow adoption at all. You might be able to legally adopt a child by the laws of the country you reside in, but not be able to ever take that child back to your home country due to the home country adoption and immigration laws.

If you must leave due to an emergency evacuation, or a health issue, or lack of funding, or any number of scenarios, what happens to the child then? Our attempts to help can sometimes bring even more harm and hurt to a child. So think through carefully the possible outcomes of your good intentions.

Are there local organizations you can trust? You don't want to give to a place that has no accountability for the helps you might offer. Research carefully before you commit yourself or your finances, especially if you are new to a culture.

Are there ways you can improve a child's situation without jeopardizing their emotional health or creating even greater problems down the road? Can you support organizations like International Justice Mission? Can you work to provide clinics for street children and impoverished mothers to teach childcare and basic sanitation? Can you help a child flourish in his home environment?

If you want to adopt a child, do your homework first. Find out what your home country's immigration and adoption laws are. Find out what your resident country's adoption laws are. Find out if there are steps you can take ahead of time to speed up the paperwork so that once you adopt, the process will go more smoothly.

Many countries are now part of the Hague Convention. Study the implications of that. Make sure you are not contributing inadvertently to a system that exploits children by using an unethical agency. Don't make promises to a child that you may not be able to keep. You may not be able to adopt a specific child who has stolen your heart. But you may be able to adopt a child who is just as needy or even more so. Most of the adoption laws, while sometimes cumbersome or even seemingly wrong in how they provide care for children, have the intention of protecting the children from those who would exploit them.

**NOTES:**

# Chapter 11 – Returning to Home Base

When it is time to go, leave things in order—relationships, financial obligations, and legal issues. As much as is up to you, don't leave with unresolved conflict or unexpressed gratitude. Pay off debts. Close out accounts. Tell people and places goodbye. Take photos. Then just get on the plane.

When returning to your home country, there are usually lots of mixed emotions. They can be very complex and difficult to process, especially if you had to leave due to sudden health, political, or other reasons. Take time to read articles, books, and blogs about re-entry issues. There are many helpful ones out there, and it will normalize the complicated feelings you face.

It is challenging that you have this whole part of your life that your family and friends do not know and understand. They are interested up to a point, but do not have the capacity to really comprehend it. So in addition to returning to old friendships, we have enjoyed seeking out ongoing relationships with internationals or others who have lived the ex-pat life. With them, there is a natural affinity and we don't have to explain ourselves.

Often, it is easy to become critical of your home culture after living overseas. If your home culture is wealthy, you feel they do not appreciate what they have. If your home culture is poor, you resent the poverty and more difficult life. If your home culture is chaotic, you might be unsettled. If your home culture is orderly, you might be bored.

Instead of looking at your home culture as "going home," try looking at it as a new culture you are entering. Do some of the Chapter 1 suggestions in reverse: Get caught up on current events, music, and trends. Read current books and watch current movies. Try to understand and accept your home citizens with patience and interest, just like you tried to understand your guest country when you first moved there. This helps make a more positive transition.

**NOTES:**

**BOOKS TO READ, WEBSITES, THOUGHTS:**

## Conclusion

Living overseas has enriched our lives incredibly. We have had some very hard times, excruciating family separations, scary situations, and uncomfortable personal stretching opportunities. We have enjoyed a rich variety of precious friendships, delicious food, beautiful scenery, and hilarious "you won't believe what happened today" episodes.

We have six children who have largely grown up overseas. In spite of those hard times, they would not trade their experiences and their unique lives for anybody else's. There are some years I would never want to repeat; yet, I would not erase them, either. It's been good. I hope that your adventures into the ex-pat lifestyle are equally as exciting and priceless!

## About the Author

Joan B. Perkins is a native of the U.S. state of Alabama. She graduated from Jacksonville State University (in Alabama) in 1982. A few weeks later, she married Bill Perkins, and they moved to Ft. Worth, Texas, where they studied at Southwestern Baptist Theological Seminary. Joan received a Master of Divinity degree in 1985.

In 1991, Joan and Bill moved overseas, and they lived and worked in an overseas setting for almost twenty-five years, including the countries of Costa Rica, Argentina, Bangladesh, India, and Thailand. They have six children, one daughter-in-law, one granddaughter, and now reside in Birmingham, Alabama. Joan can be contacted at perkins.joan.b@gmail.com.

Made in the USA
Middletown, DE
24 April 2022